DEDICATION

This book is dedicated to my
grandfather, Walker Dee Wallace,
author, without whom my talents may
have never been sown. To my mother,
Dot Parish, whose love and strength I
have cherished. To my children, Tara
Parish Matfey and Justin Walker Parish,
for their unconditional love and
continued support of me through all my
adversities. And to my precious wife,
Cathi Snow Parish, without whom my
life would not be complete, nor my walk
in faith, or this book, possible.

Kevin and Cathi Parish

TABLE OF CONTENTS

Title	Page

Title	Page

ACKNOWLEDGEMENTS

I'd first like to thank my wife, Cathi Parish, for her patience, encouragement and latitude in allowing me to write my words. I praise her for her reading, re-reading, proofing, editing and keeping me fed and happy, both physically and spiritually. I couldn't have done this without you, sweetie! You have done so much for me that I would need to write another book just to cover it. I love you my precious wife!

I especially want to acknowledge and thank Lisa K. Eaker for her friendship, encouragement and helping me to share my works. She singlehandedly got me started on WordPress and has continued to advise and mentor me. I also wish to thank Scott Eaker (Lisa's husband) for his friendship and support and being a walking example of faith.

Michele Jones Arnett helped me see that my talent for writing may lay somewhere other than writing short stories, thus releasing my poetry to flourish. Thank you so much, Michele!

My precious children, Tara Parish Matfey and Justin Walker Parish read so many of my early songs and poems that I cannot begin to thank them enough for their encouraging words. You two are truly a blessing to me. I love you! Thank you for putting up with me and always being there when I need you!

FOREWARD

I decided that it was not wisdom that enabled poets to write their poetry, but a kind of instinct or inspiration, such as you find in seers and prophets who deliver all their sublime messages without knowing in the least what they mean.
Socrates

Each time Kevin showed me a new poem, shared a story or some lyrics to a song that had yet to be set to music, he told me he didn't know what the piece meant. Genuinely asking what I thought, not from an evaluation perspective, but eagerly sharing his words, or more accurately the words that flowed from his fingers to a keyboard without what he considered intervention from him, sharing with wonder and astonishment that **somehow** he had created **something,** he waited for my reaction. To say that our writing styles are different is an understatement. I typically think and overthink and edit and delete while he lets the words come and dutifully records them. Yet his trust that they will come, that there is meaning, that he is bound by his faith to get these messages out into the world, is exactly the childlike trust that Jesus asked us all to live out. While his writing is fast and never forced, I need time to consider and process and slowly explore what each offering means to me. I find the same is true about the psalms, words spoken with passion and urgency yet profoundly alive and evolving and ever open to interpretation. I invite the reader to enter this collection with that same openness, that same wonder, that exact hopefulness as Kevin exhibited each time he sat before his laptop. I cannot tell you what YOU will find here but I know that God has a message for each of us in this assemblage.

I am grateful for the opportunity to call this man of faith my friend, to be allowed a glimpse into that holy time when God speaks directly to him, to wander in the gift of words that come when a faithful servant dares to stop and listen, and ultimately, to know that what we discover is meant truly for each of us.

Lisa Eaker
Patches of Light, Pieces of Grace
(www.lisaeaker.com)

A BLANK PIECE OF PAPER

It's just a blank piece of paper
For anyone to see
A blank piece of paper
Is magical to me
Upon the white
I write in black
Of gifts received each day
On a blank piece of paper
I give praise - I give praise

A blank piece of paper
Is where I'll write some poetry
A blank piece of paper
So that all of you might see
What the Spirit does within
This common, common man
On a blank piece of paper

From my heart - to the great I Am

Thoughts

_____

_____

_____

_____

_____

_____

_____

_____

_____

ACCOUNTABLE

Count my soul as one marked for glory.

Count my life as one that lives.

Count my heart as one filled with love.

Count my hands as those that give.

Hold yourself to a higher purpose.

Hold yourself to a cross before you.

Hold yourself with respect for others.

Hold yourself and hold to virtue.

Gather in those who are broken.

Gather in those who have lost their way.

Gather in those who forgot their
purpose.

Gather in those and with them, pray!

Thoughts

_____

_____

_____

_____

_____

_____

_____

_____

_____

_____

ALIMONY

The battle was fought

Long, long ago

A war was won

To save my soul

A sacrifice

Upon a cross

He bled for me

And paid the cost

The alimony

To keep us free

Even for

A wretch like me

Thoughts

_____

_____

_____

_____

_____

_____

_____

_____

_____

_____

CALVARY

Even with her torrent of tears
She couldn't wash away
What happened there on Calvary
That sad and bloody day

A thief and robber on each side
Her son upon a cross to die
His precious name was Jesus Christ
The crowd it shouted, "Crucify!"

Those who'd followed him around
Where were they now
Could they be found
His final breath - They aren't around
His blood it runs upon the ground

Thoughts

_____

_____

_____

_____

_____

_____

_____

_____

_____

CHERISH

Cherish and nourish my faith, oh Lord

In the way it is meant to be

Break down the walls

Of doubt and despair

Care for this treasure, called me

Open my hands to help another

Open my heart that I might love

Let Your Holy Spirit fill this vessel

That I might shine forth

Your light from above

Thoughts

_____

_____

_____

_____

_____

_____

_____

_____

COLLECT IN ME

Collect these chains
That bind my heart.
Collect this sorrow
That broke it apart.
Take all my gold,
Silver and my worth.
Then find in me
The reason for rebirth.

Collect these words
That bring me down.
Collect this breath
And in me rebound.
Open my eyes
Once again to see.
The one true path
Where You want me to be.

"But by the grace of God
I am what I am..."
Let these words sink into me
Where my value can be found.
Collect in me...

Thoughts

_____

_____

_____

_____

_____

_____

_____

_____

_____

_____

CONFLICTED

Conflicted!

A testimonial to those of faltered or

undiscovered faith.

Where is my mettle, O Lord?

What will You have me do?

The mountain used to seem so high,

But I ascended because of You!

And in return for what You revealed in

me

I promised Your words from my lips.

Yet, here I stand before this crowd

Hypocrisy, firmly grips.

Beautiful surrender in these offered words

That are endowed within me to say.

But the Evil one has plans of his own

As he attempts them here today.

Hear my prayer, oh Holy God,

And show them what You can do.

With such as me

Unworthy, yet free,

From a heart that belongs to You.

Thoughts

CRUCIFIED

Something drew me to the hill.
I heard shouting and crying in the
distance.
There was something of great loss
there.

I sensed it in the air itself.
What is this invisible urging that draws
me onward?
There seems to be a crowd around the
other side of that hill.

Before me, I see something that stops
me and I drop to my knees.
I see a man on a cross.

He has been crucified.

Inside my heart I feel a stirring of deep regret.

Who is this person that has affected me so?

Without realizing I begin to cry as my face turns upwards.

"God, here I am!"

Thoughts

DIVINE THE TRINITY

The Lord my God

Loves me more

Much more than I can see

Powerful, powerful

In accord

Divine the Trinity

Thoughts

ETERNITY

Cradle my hands in yours

Kiss them one more time

The sun will rise

And the sun will fall

As my time has come to die

But do not shed yours tears, oh no

Not for a loss

Not for me

My true life is about to begin

With my God in Eternity

Thoughts

_____

_____

_____

_____

_____

_____

_____

_____

_____

_____

Beauty in Blue

FEEBLE HANDS

Why would I ever live in fear
My Lord, my God I plead thee, hear
Prayers I'm lifting with feeble hands
Shaken and cold
Best laid plans
But solace waits upon the glade
Delivered was the promise made
For He sits high on God's right side
Fulfilled the dream
His heart His pride

For all of us to keep our faith
Believe in His ever-present grace
Bowed head and remember
What will comfort me
Found in Psalm 23

Thoughts

FORGIVENESS

As he lay there beaten where he had

been robbed

Of, not only his valuables, but also his

shoes

He tried to look up through closed,

swollen eyes,

Bleeding nose and lips from the abuse

Not able to remember

A word they said

When they beat him there

And left him for dead

He managed to pull up

Upon his knees

To pray a prayer

Of forgiveness, please

"Forgive those who trespassed

Against me this night

And grant them the wisdom

To see what is right

Bring them happiness

And fill in the void

Where they see destruction

Let them see joy

If this is Your will, Lord,

Please - let it be

I ask this in Jesus' name – not for me"

Thoughts

HEAVEN'S DOOR

They were well-worn callused hands

That was always daddy's way

He taught me how to throw a ball

And fold my hands to pray

I think about him all the time

He passed some years ago

And how he always said, "I love you!"

Then off to work he'd go

He rarely showed the sadness

That must have been behind his eyes

Some nights I'd wake and hear a sound

I know my daddy cries

But he's much better off today

Then he ever was before

And I know he'll be there waiting

When I get to Heaven's door

Thoughts

HIS CALL

Love is the gift
That was given to man
The ultimate sacrifice
So we'd understand

Nothing is greater
Than what Jesus did
There on the cross
Innocent of sin

Yet, He was convicted
For breaking the law
The arrogance of man
Deceitful and small

But God had a plan
To temper this place
Vicious the crowd
To drown in disgrace

Yet, His rules are simple
For one and for all
Love God
Love your neighbor
Answer His call

Thoughts

_____

_____

_____

_____

_____

_____

_____

_____

_____

HOPE

The glint from a crystal

Hanging in the window

Reminded me of hope

And the promise made long ago

"I am the light of the world"

Jesus spoke to the crowd

The Son of man on earth

In whom God was proud

"I am the way

And the truth

And the life," said He

Crucified at the age of 33

And, so I keep faith

Wrapped up tight in my soul

For the One who died for me

Forever made me whole

Thoughts

Dazzle

I AM

I am the Rock

That provides a firm foundation.

I am the Light

That darkness fears the most.

I am the Blood

That was shed for your salvation.

I am the Way

That provides you eternal life.

Thoughts

IF

If my heart breaks

Help me become stronger, not

calloused, because of it.

If I misunderstand

Help me see through their eyes and

their truth.

If I judge

Let my shame become my catalyst of

knowledge to teach others.

If I fall

Let me have the courage to pull others

up when I stand.

If I lose

Gift me with wisdom to see why and try

again.

When I die

Let the worth of my living serve the lives

of all those who knew me.

Thoughts

IF I AM LAST

What if I am last?

What will it mean about my life?

Am I the same as those before me,

Or unique in my design?

How beautiful the tapestry

All the colors of mankind...

Still, I wonder as I sit here

When it comes my time to die...

Will I be last and final witness,

To this temporary home?

Mother Nature in her grandeur

Who will marvel at her soul?

As the closing curtain falls

And the sun makes its final pass

How wonderful this life has been

So what - if I am last...

Thoughts

INTOXICATED

I want to overindulge

I want to be intoxicated

With the Holy Spirit

I want to attract the attention of others

Let them look upon me in wonder

Let them seek out what I have

Fill their hearts with desire

To flood their lives with the joy they see

in me

Give them the words to ask me what I

know

Give them the hope that you've given
me

Let us go out together into the world and
spread Your word

Let us go out into the world and shine in
your Spirit

Let our jubilation be contagious and
spread

Amen

Thoughts

_____

_____

_____

_____

_____

_____

_____

LIGHT

Cast me into the living sculpture

Of what You would have me to be

Bring those souls who are lost in this

world

To the light You would shine in me

A beacon of peace and hope and love

That this mortal servant can give

To begin anew

In the hope of You

So that their light too can live

Thoughts

_____

_____

_____

_____

_____

_____

_____

_____

Prayer in Purple

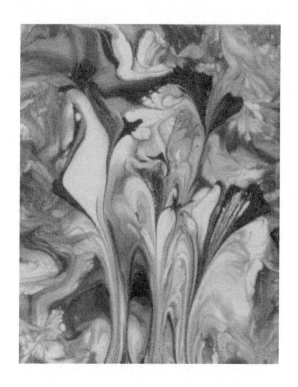

MARY

How was I to know
At such a tender age
When he gave to me, his heart
That faith would be the wage

We were so in love
The future looking bright
Then a miracle within me
Happened overnight

All the hopes and dreams
I had when just a girl
Suddenly, were questioning
As this saga did unfurl

But when the angel said to me
"You carry the Son of man"
Who was I to query him
The words of one so grand

"Many will look upon you
And speak words harsh and cruel
But they will never understand
The servant's heart in you"

Now, I look back on the journey
Of just 33 years
My son said it would happen
But still, I shed the tears

His legacy will forever be
His promise to the world
He set the table for you and me
My God
My Son
My Lord

Thoughts

_____

_____

_____

_____

_____

_____

_____

_____

_____

_____

MY OFFER

In the words of the Father

I offer you peace

In the words of the Spirit

I offer you knowledge

In the words of Jesus

I offer you love

Thoughts

NEW DAWN

Blessings cascaded down the mountain
Spreading far and wide across the land
Heaven was behind this glorious deed
God, The Holy Spirit and Son of Man

Beautiful singing was heard all around
As the world bore witness to this wonder
Trumpets could be heard
A pleasing sound
Beneath the rolling thunder

Redemption, salvation and confession
aplenty
From the lips of the sinners and the
saved
The Trinity has come down to earth
As a new dawn crests on the day

Thoughts

_____

_____

_____

_____

_____

_____

_____

_____

PAUL

No light is brighter

Than the one upon that road

Every single dream I lost

Every single hope

To those I persecuted, yeah

The ones I would have stoned

They are the brothers I never knew

My family and my home

Never would I look again

Upon the life I lived

But only to the future

The one that Christ did give

In Him I found the meaning

Of what my life should be

Until I die

I will not deny

The Savior who saved me

Thoughts

_____

_____

_____

_____

_____

_____

_____

_____

PERSEVERANCE

Her name was Sorrow.

And, she had lost her way.

Riding on hopes of tomorrow.

Snagging doubts along the way.

A sad, sad ugly lullaby...

Playing in her heart.

Always weighing down.

Tearing her apart.

His name was Gentle.

The world in his hand.

An oyster with a million pearls

And giving all he can.

When one day, something missing,

He didn't know what it could be.

A lullaby played in his mind.

And a face he longed to see.

Rounding corners on the sidewalk
Of a crowded city street.
Crashing in to one another
But he caught her with his reach.
And looking up into his eyes
A new song played in her heart.
The woman he had dreamt about
Was there within his arms.

Happily, ever after
Isn't just a fairy tale.
Anytime, it can come rushing in
Like winds upon a sail.
For everyone there's someone
Who longs to hold them near.
Even in a lonely heart
Hope can persevere.

Thoughts

_____

_____

_____

_____

_____

_____

_____

_____

_____

_____

Blended Flowers

PRAYERS

When I woke up this morning

And looked at my spouse...

I smiled!

Sometimes...

God really does answer prayers!

Thoughts

_____

_____

_____

_____

_____

_____

_____

_____

_____

_____

_____

PROSPERITY

God, please grant me
The innocence and spirit of a child
To see through eyes of purity
A world of hope, and love, and trust

Christ once walked among us
In a world that we defiled
With falsities and idolatries
Yet we remained above the dust

Holy Spirit infuse us all
So, our blinded eyes might see
To begin again beyond our sin
Trusting your prosperity

Thoughts

_____

_____

_____

_____

_____

_____

_____

_____

RECONCILED

I rise with the Son

Each and every day

My eyes are open and clear

And I pray they will stay that way

To believe in the promise

That Jesus made to you and me

Is to know that I'm protected

And chosen for eternity

I think about the virtue

That He showed upon the cross

The world had gained a Savior

And then paid a heavy cost

But the Father gladly gave to us

In the sacrifice of His child

That we might know a better way

And thus, be reconciled

Thoughts

_____

_____

_____

_____

_____

_____

_____

_____

_____

S.A.V.I.O.R.

Submission is what frees me

Absolution is what He gave me

Value for others is what feeds me

Immanence is I believe of Him

Omnipotence is His and His alone

Redemption is what I find through Christ

Jesus

Thoughts

_____

_____

_____

_____

_____

_____

_____

_____

_____

_____

SIMPLE WORDS

Heaven help the hapless soul
Who knows not how to live.
Heaven help the homeless man
Who gave all he could give.
Father, help me open up
These eyes that do not see.
Brother won't you lend a hand
With this burden that I bring?
And when my time has come to rest
To heaven shall I go?
For in my heart I've tried to carry
Faith and love and hope.
In this, I take heart my friend
In the words I've often read.
"For God so loved the World..."
These simple words that John said.

Thoughts

Birth of a Galaxy

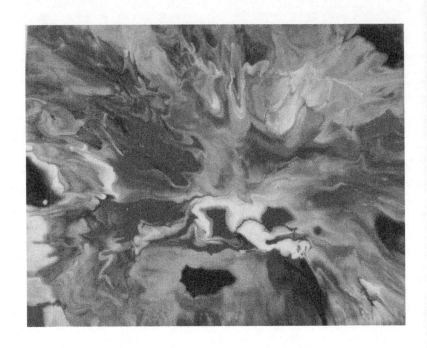

SPARROWS

I see You in the sparrows

In the branches of the trees

I see You in the heard of deer

In the butterflies and bees

I see You in the sunny sky

In the spectrum of the rainbow

I feel Your love so deep inside

You are the only Way I know

Thoughts

_____

_____

_____

_____

_____

_____

_____

_____

_____

STAGES

I watched her pray today

Then I held her hand while she cried.

I watched her read today

Then I held her hand while she cried.

I watched her laugh today

Then I held her hand while she cried.

I watched her die today...

Then I held her close while I cried.

Thoughts

_____

_____

_____

_____

_____

_____

_____

_____

_____

_____

STRIFE

Oh Lord, how my heart aches

As I look back on my life

Of wreckage and lies

Dear God, guide and open me

To the splendor of Your grace

And forgive days gone by

Precious Jesus, such sacrifice

And, yet I have not obeyed

Though you gave up your life

Holy Spirit, fill in this void

So, I might make you proud

In the release of this strife

Thoughts

_____
_____
_____
_____
_____
_____
_____
_____
_____
_____

THE FATHER

The tears of a father

Hurt the most

A dampening of strength on display

And pride of the mother

The loving host

To comfort the needs of the day

Who was there

When the Son who died

Gave His all for us

A loving God

Who is filled with pride

Give thanks, and drink from the cup

Thoughts

_____

_____

_____

_____

_____

_____

_____

_____

_____

THE SON

When the Son shined down on me
I had to hide my swollen eyes
Though I prayed that I could witness
Him
He took me by surprise

Oh, and how my body trembled
Kneeling there within His grace
I felt a gentle hand upon me
As He knelt to see my face

There was a rush of exaltation
From every part of me
Never had I known such love
Perhaps my eyes had never seen

And so, so very gently He helped me to
my feet
Then He put his arms around me
And the smell of Him was sweet

He told me that He loved me
And He told me He was proud
His words of adoration
Had me riding on a cloud

Then He smiled and left me there
But I knew I'd never be alone
For when the Son came down that day
It was upon my life He'd shone

Thoughts

_____

_____

_____

_____

_____

_____

_____

_____

_____

Red Galaxy

THE TOUCH

My shoulders ache from the weight I
carry
My legs burn with added strain
Walking, walking, walking forever
Why must I bear all this pain

I see others moving in the same
direction
To them I offer prayers of hope
Yet in myself I disregard
As I trudge ahead conveying this load

A fellow traveler then offered me
The words I needed to hear the most
From his lips to my heart a prayer was
lifted
I then felt the touch of the Holy Ghost

Thoughts

_____
_____
_____
_____
_____
_____
_____
_____
_____

WHAT WORDS MAY COME

A lifetime
Of not knowing
Where my talents lie
Afraid to look
Afraid to ask
Never knowing why

But, slowly
As I found my way
Turning more to prayer
I learned a lesson
I'm not alone
My God is always there

And this I took
Straight to my heart
Giving it to Him

And let go

Of the pride I had

Confessing to my sin

His ever-loving kindness

Has built in me

A sum

Adding to

The scripts I write

And call - What Words May Come

Thoughts

WHEN I COME HOME

When I come home to You,

Will I come home whole?

Will I have wings like other angels,

Or will they be broken like my soul?

I never made it up the mountain,

As I was too afraid to climb.

When I come home You, my Lord

Will I be rescued from this life?

Hazard, is my middle name

My first name is Beware.

Never have I trusted, no,

Not another could I bear.

So, maybe it is fitting, yeah,

And You won't let me in.

If my wings are made of wax

Then I will fall back down again.

When I come home to You,

Will I come home whole?

Will I have wings like other angels,

Or will they be broken like my soul?

I never made it up the mountain,

As I was too afraid to climb.

When I come home You, my Lord

Will I be rescued from this life?

What is that light a-shining,

And my skin like electricity?

This is a feeling that I've never known,

With open eyes I now can see.

I am not forsaken, no,

Perhaps my heart was just confused.

For I am filled now with the Spirit

And my life has been infused.

When I come home to You,

Will I come home whole?

Will I have wings like other angels,

Or will they be broken like my soul?

I never made it up the mountain,

As I was too afraid to climb.

When I come home You, my Lord

Will I be rescued from this life?

Thoughts

WITH HANDS HELD HIGH

With hands held high

I will praise You from the mountain

With head bowed low

I will pray with all my being

With folded hands

I will teach my children

The power of Your love

In water Holy

We will baptize

And be seen

With hands held high...

Thoughts

WRITTEN WORDS

I admit the folly of my pride,
And that's where it hit first.
Actions that I took in stride
And for these -
I was cursed.

Simple are the rules to follow
To one and all be kind.
Selfishness draws you to the shallows
Of haplessness – salty - brined.

You cannot unwrite the written words
Scribed upon your life.
Ever evolving, ever forward
Live and learn –
Lock out the strife.

Thoughts

Bonus

This is a dream I had…

HOW I DIED AND FOUND SOLACE

(A true story)

It's a long winding, treacherous dirt and gravel mountain road strewn with large boulders all along its edges. The sides drop steeply as the tall pines stretch towards the heavens. I see their tops blown and bristled against the distance in some places as we descend with ever increasing speed. It's beginning to scare me along with everyone else in the car. I'm sitting in the front passenger seat while three others are crowded together in the back. We're driving entirely too fast, and for whatever reason, our driver believes she can maintain control. Why she doesn't slow down no one in the car knows. With a cry of fear and terror, I beg her to slow down before we reach the next curve and the large boulders that are our only means of preventing us from flying off the edge and into the abyss. She loses control and we careen into, onto and over the boulders. We all scream with terror and fear in anticipation of the long journey down and our inevitable death.

The screaming ceases, if only for a brief moment, as we realize we haven't crashed down the 400-500 feet to the ground near the speck of a stream flowing there. I note that we have somehow, miraculously landed atop a towering pine. Turning to the group I tell them to hold on as we are about to lose our perch. Down, down, down… The screaming rings in my ears as we whirl in a plunging spiral towards the earth and death. It's over! The car is crushed nearly flat as it landed top down with full impact.

I'm aware of people milling around the car and paramedics tending to my friends. I'm being pulled from the car even as I watch from a short distance. My body is bloody and crushed. I mutter aloud that I don't understand how we weren't all killed. We couldn't have possibly survived that kind of impact. It dawned on me that I had been praying all the way down for God to save us or take us home. I prayed that my children and family would not suffer too much with the burden of losing their father, husband, brother in such a manner. I then realize that I am watching this scene play out in front of me and I am not a survivor. I died…

As I turn to look at the person standing next to me he nods his head in affirmation of my epiphany. A sense of relief rushes over me as goosebumps stand up and fall back again all over my body. I'm dead, but I'm alive and unafraid. I know I am safe and in the presence of Jesus. This short time for me on earth is complete and I will now go home and see my dad and grandparents again. There is solace in this feeling that I cannot explain in this short work. I only know that the Holy

Spirit descended upon me in a dream that changed my life forever. My soul is claimed, safe and I'm okay.

Kevin D. Parish

Thoughts

Additional information for Kevin's work…

Writing

Other literary works that Kevin has published can be found on his WordPress site.

https://www.whatwordsmaycome.com

https://www.wordpress.com/view/whatwordsmaycome.com

Art

In addition to Kevin's written works he also produces and sells acrylic artwork.
What Arts May Come

https://www.etsy.com/shop/WhatArtsMayCome

Made in the USA
Monee, IL
18 July 2021